Python Crash Course: A Hands-On Introduction to Programming

Eric Sindeu

Published by Eric Sindeu, 2024.

PYTHON CRASH COURSE: A HANDS-ON INTRODUCTION TO PROGRAMMING

BY ERIC SINDEU

Python Crash Course: A HANDS-ON INTRODUCTION TO PROGRAMMING

By Eric SindeU

DISCLAIMER

This book is intended for educational purposes only and should not be considered a substitute for professional advice. The information provided within does not constitute legal, financial, or medical advice of any kind.

While every effort has been made to ensure the accuracy and completeness of the information presented, the author and publisher assume no responsibility for any errors or omissions. Readers are encouraged to verify any information presented herein through independent research and consult with qualified professionals as needed.

The software code and examples provided in this book are illustrative only and may not be suitable for all purposes. In order to promote ethical coding, the mention *"Use code with caution."* is attached to every code example. Readers are responsible for understanding the risks and limitations of using code and should test and modify it as necessary for their specific applications.

The reader assumes all risks associated with the use of the information and code provided in this book, and neither the author nor the publisher shall be liable for any damages resulting from their use.

This book may contain links to external websites and resources. The author and publisher are not responsible for the content or accuracy of any external information and do not endorse any views expressed or products or services offered thereon.

By using this book, you agree to the terms and conditions of this disclaimer.

All tools, functions and resources pertaining to Python programming are labeled in **blue.**

Prologue

e are currently witnessing the digital revolution after the industrial revolution of the 1900s. Our society has been completely transformed over the years with the ever evolving technologies in big data, artificial intelligence, cloud computing, cryptocurrencies etc..

There's a growing need for coders to sustain this growth, and this book will help you on your journey to master the language of Python[1], a language designed by *Guido Van Russum* of the **Python Software Foundation** with a first appearance on February 20th 1991. Throughout this book we will have a practical approach to Python programming, so a working computer with an internet connectivity will be optimal.

Pixels of Potential

The pixelated cursor blinked on the black screen, taunting me with its blank promise. A canvas of possibility, yes, but how to fill it? It wasn't the paintbrush I feared, nor the clay, but the keyboard, its keys silent instruments in a language I longed to speak. Code felt like a secret handshake with machines, a hidden alphabet holding the power to bend the digital world to my will.

My journey began with hesitant clicks, tentative steps into a maze of commands and loops. Numbers became poetry, strings of characters transformed into spells, and algorithms spun worlds before my eyes. With each line of code, I built bridges across uncharted landscapes, crafting solutions in the flickering firelight of the screen.

And it wasn't just about mastering functions or conquering syntax. It was about unlocking infinite possibilities. Imagine conjuring music from algorithms, painting emotions with pixels, sculpting narratives from data. Imagine breathing life into robots, teaching machines to learn, and whispering commands that echo across the silicon valleys of the digital universe.

This book is your blueprint, your decoder ring for the language of computers. Within its pages, you'll find not just the technical blueprints, but the spark of a revolution. You'll learn to read the hidden narratives in every website, decode the secrets behind every game, and rewrite the scripts that govern the digital world around you.

No longer a passive consumer, you'll become a **creator**, an **architect** of the unseen. So, come, turn the page, pick up your keyboard, and let's etch our dreams into the digital canvas. Remember, every line of code is a pixel of potential, a stepping stone on your path to becoming the weaver of your own digital destiny.

1.

Python Basics

Welcome, intrepid adventurer, to the exciting world of Python programming! In this chapter, we'll dive headfirst into the language's fundamental building blocks, equipping you with the tools to craft your first lines of code. Fear not, even if you've never ventured into this digital realm before, we'll navigate it together step-by-step, transforming curious clicks into confident commands.

Setting Up Your Coding Playground

Before we unleash the power of Python, let's prepare our environment. First, download and install Python from **https://www.python.org/downloads/**. Once installed, choose your weapon of choice , a code editor where you'll type your code. Popular options include **Visual Studio Code, PyCharm**, or even the built-in **IDLE** that comes with Python. With your editor ready, open a new file – your digital canvas awaits!

Hello, World!: Your First Python Song

Let's begin with a classic introduction. Type the following line into your editor:

```Python
print("Hello, world!")
```
Use code with caution.

Save the file (save the world!), then run it. Witness the magic! Your code comes to life, printing the joyous greeting on your screen. You've just written your first Python program! Celebrate, for this simple line is the first spark that ignites a world of possibilities.

Numbers and Words: The Building Blocks

Now, let's venture deeper into the realm of data. Numbers, the builders of the digital world, can be expressed in Python through integers (whole numbers like 10 or -25) and floats (numbers with decimals like 3.14 or 9.87). Words, the storytellers of code, are represented by strings enclosed in quotes (single or double): "Python is awesome!" or 'What a beautiful day!'.

Play with these data types. Experiment by adding numbers, concatenating strings, and even mixing them like a digital chef:

```Python
age = 25
message = "My age is " + str(age) # Combining a string and a number
print(message) # Output: "My age is 25"
```
Use code with caution.

The Symphony of Operators

Just as music flourishes from notes and their relationships, code dances to the rhythm of operators. They combine data or perform calculations, adding (+), subtracting (-), multiplying (*), and dividing (/). Remember the order of operations (PEMDAS)[2] so your calculations sing the right tune!

Explore further with comparison operators: == for equality, != for difference, < for less than, and > for greater than. These gates guide your code down different paths, like musical junctions leading to new melodies.

```Python
score1 = 75
score2 = 80
passed = score1 > 60 # True if score1 is greater than 60
if passed:
print("Congratulations! You passed!")
else:
print("Keep practicing, you'll get there!")
```
Use code with caution.

Variables: Storing Your Treasures

Imagine a magical bag that holds any valuable you come across on your coding journey. That's a variable! Use its name to access its treasures later. Assign data to a variable using the = sign:

```
Python
name = "Alice"
age = 30
is_coding = True # Assigning boolean values (True or False)
```
Use code with caution.

Variables make your code reusable and dynamic. Call upon them throughout your program, weaving them into your digital tapestry.

Loops and Conditions: The Rhythm of Repetition

Sometimes, tasks require repetition, like plucking the same string on a guitar multiple times to create a rhythm. In Python, loops automate this, iterating over sequences of data. The for loop plays a melody of instructions for each item in a list:

```
Python
fruits = ["apple", "banana", "orange"]
for fruit in fruits:
print(f"I love eating {fruit}!")
```
Use code with caution.

Conditional statements act like musical switches, directing your code down different paths. The **if** statement, like a conductor's raised baton, guides execution based on a condition:

```
Python
score = 90
if score >= 90:
print("Excellent work! You aced the test!")
else:
```

```
print("Keep studying, you can do even better!")
```
Use code with caution.

Beyond the Basics: A Glimpse of Possibilities

This chapter is just the first spark in your Python journey. Soon, you'll build complex functions, manipulate data structures like lists and dictionaries, and even create interactive programs like games or websites.

Remember, practice is the secret sauce! Experiment, explore, and most importantly, have fun! Dive into online tutorials, tackle coding challenges, and connect.

2
Variables and Data Types

Welcome back, fellow adventurers! In Chapter 1, we laid the foundation for our Python journey. Now, let's dive deeper into the building blocks of every program: variables and data types. These powerful tools will allow us to store information, manipulate it, and ultimately craft complex and dynamic code.

The Magic of Variables: Naming Your Treasures

Imagine a vast library, each book carefully labeled with a title. Variables are like those titles, giving names to the data we use in our programs. These names act as handles, allowing us to easily access and modify the information they hold.

```
Python
name = "Alice"
age = 30
is_coding = True
Use code with caution.
```

Here, we've declared three variables: "**name**" holds a string (Alice), "**age**" stores an integer (30), and "**is_coding**" keeps track of a boolean value (**True**). Remember, naming conventions in Python use lowercase letters and underscores (**snake_case**), making your code clear and consistent.

A Spectrum of Data Types: Storing Diverse Treasures

Think of a library holding not just books, but pictures, maps, and even musical scores. Similarly, Python offers a variety of data types to store different kinds of information:

- Numbers: Whole numbers (integers) like 10 or -5, and decimal numbers (floats) like 3.14 or 9.87.

- Strings: Collections of characters enclosed in quotes, representing text like "Python is awesome!" or 'It's a beautiful day!'.

- Booleans: Values representing True or False, like a yes/no switch in your code.

Each data type has its own characteristics and operations. You can add numbers, concatenate strings, and even compare values based on their data types.

Casting Spells: Transforming Data Types

Sometimes, you might need to change the form of your data, like transmuting a map into a written description. Python allows you to cast spells called type conversions to transform data between types:

```
Python
age_string = str(30) # Convert an integer (30) to a string ("30")
decimal_point = float(7) # Convert an integer (7) to a float (7.0)
is_even = age % 2 == 0 # Convert a division remainder (0) to a boolean (True)
```
Use code with caution.

These conversions open up new possibilities in your code, allowing you to combine and manipulate data in different ways.

Arrays and Lists: Keeping Your Treasures Organized

Imagine a treasure chest overflowing with jewels. Arrays and lists are like those chests, storing collections of data in an ordered sequence. You can access specific items using their position (index) starting from 0.

```
Python
friends = ["Alice", "Bob", "Charlie"]
print(friends[1]) # Output: Bob (the second friend)
numbers = [3, 5, 7, 9]
numbers.append(11) # Add a new item to the end of the list
for number in numbers:
print(number * 2) # Double each number in the list
```
Use code with caution.

Lists offer flexibility, allowing you to add, remove, or modify items as your program needs.

Dictionaries: Unlocking Hidden Vaults

Remember that secret door in the library leading to a hidden chamber? Dictionaries act like those doors, storing data under unique keys instead of ordered positions. These keys allow you to access information instantly, like retrieving a specific book by its title.

```
Python
person = {"name": "Alice", "age": 30, "job": "Programmer"}
print(person["name"]) # Output: Alice
person["age"] = 31 # Update the age value
```
Use code with caution.

Dictionaries are powerful tools for organizing complex data and building rich, interlinked structures within your programs.

Unleashing the Power: Combining Types and Operations

As you gain confidence with variables and data types, remember, the magic lies in their fusion. Combine different types, use operators to manipulate them, and leverage loops and conditional statements to control their flow. With these tools, you'll construct complex programs, unlock hidden insights from data, and create digital experiences that inspire and amaze.

This is just a glimpse into the fascinating world of variables and data types. Keep exploring, experiment with different combinations, and let your code become a tapestry woven with threads of data and logic. The possibilities are endless!

Remember:

- Choose meaningful names for your variables.
- Understand the strengths and limitations of each data type.
- Practice casting spells with type conversions.
- Organize your data using arrays, lists, and dictionaries.

3

operators and expressions

In our previous chapters, we laid the foundation with variables and data types. Now, we embark on a deeper journey into the heart of Python, realm of operators and expressions. These are the tools that breathe life into your data, allowing you to perform calculations, make decisions, and ultimately express your intentions within your code.

The Symphony of Operators: Combining the Notes

Just as music arises from the interplay of notes and symbols, Python code dances to the rhythm of operators. These magical symbols guide your data, performing calculations, comparisons, and manipulations:

- Arithmetic operators: +, -, *, /, // (integer division), % (modulo) for basic math operations.

- Comparison operators: ==, !=, <, >, <=, >= for testing relationships between values.

- Logical operators: **and, or, not** for combining comparisons and creating complex conditions.

Remember the order of operations, PEMDAS, just like a conductor's baton dictating which musical notes play first. Use parentheses to ensure your calculations follow the desired order.

Example:
```Python
total_apples = 10
apples_eaten = 3
apples_left = total_apples - apples_eaten
is_enough_left = apples_left >= 5 # Combining subtraction and comparison
```
Use code with caution.

Expressions: Weaving the Melody

Imagine crafting a musical phrase by combining notes and rests. Expressions do the same with data and operators, forming units of calculation or comparison. These expressions act as building blocks, paving the way for complex logic within your code.

Example:

```
Python
average_speed = (distance_traveled / time_taken)
print(f"Your average speed was {average_speed} kilometers per hour.")
```

Use code with caution.

Here, we combine variables, operators, and even a function call to build a meaningful expression that calculates and displays the average speed.

Conditional Statements: Branching Paths in the Melody

Sometimes, music takes unexpected turns, branching into different sections based on dynamics or mood. Similarly, conditional statements allow your code to follow different paths based on the outcome of an expression. The ever-reliable **if** statement acts like a musical fork in the road, leading your program down alternative avenues based on a condition.

Example:

```
Python
if age >= 18:
print("You are eligible to vote!")
else:
print("You will be eligible to vote in", 18 - age, "years.")
```

Use code with caution.

In this code, the **if** statement checks if the age is greater than or equal to 18, printing different messages depending on the condition.

Loops: Repeating the Rhythm

Music often employs repetition to build tension or create catchy grooves. In Python, loops offer a similar power, allowing you to execute a block of code multiple times based on a specific condition. The **for** loop iterates over a sequence of data, like a musician playing each note in a melody.

Example:

```Python
fruits = ["apple", "banana", "orange"]
for fruit in fruits:
print(f"I love eating {fruit}!")
```

Use code with caution.

Here, the loop iterates over the **fruits** list, printing a message for each item within the sequence.

Beyond the Basics: Advanced Expressions and Logic

Remember, this is just the beginning of your exploration into the realm of operators and expressions. As you progress, you'll encounter complex mathematical functions, logical operators like **not, in** and **or**, and even conditional expressions that combine comparisons and calculations within a single line. Embrace the challenge, practice your craft, and soon you'll be composing symphonies of code that manipulate data, solve problems, and create anything your imagination can conjure.

Remember:

- Master the order of operations (PEMDAS).
- Build complex expressions by combining data, operators, and functions.
- Use conditional statements to control the flow of your code.
- Leverage loops to automate repetitive tasks.
- Explore advanced operators and expressions to enhance your code's power.

With these tools at your fingertips, the possibilities are endless! Go forth, adventurer, and weave your own unique melody in the language of Python!

4

control flow

Welcome back, Captain Coder! In our previous chapters, we built the ship: variables, data types, operations, and expressions, ready to navigate the digital seas. Now, we raise the sails of control flow, charting a course through our programs and steering them towards their destinations.

Control flow gives your code the ability to make decisions, react to conditions, and choose different paths based on the data it encounters. It's like having a map and compass, ensuring your program reaches its goal efficiently and effectively.

The Mighty 'if' Statement: Choosing Your Route

Imagine encountering a fork in the road while sailing. The trusty **if** statement acts as your compass, letting you pick a direction based on a specific condition.

Python

```python
if age >= 18:
print("Welcome aboard, adult passenger!")
# Code for adults...
else:
print("Ahoy, young matey! Enjoy the kid's zone!")
# Code for children...
```

Use code with caution.

Here, the **if** statement checks if the passenger's age is 18 or above. If true, they board the adult section; if false, they head to the kid's zone.

The 'else' and 'elif': Exploring Alternative Routes

Sometimes, life (and code) throws you curveballs. The **else** statement acts as your emergency plan, taking control if none of your **if** conditions are met. And for those unforeseen turns, the **elif** (else if) is your handy navigator, allowing you to check additional conditions and adjust your course accordingly.

```Python
if skill_level == "expert":
print("Prepare for a challenging voyage!")
elif skill_level == "intermediate":
print("Let's set sail for moderate seas!")
else:
print("Relax, enjoy the calm waters, matey.")
```
Use code with caution.

This code checks the user's sailing skill level, offering different experiences based on their choice.

Loops: Repeating the Journey

Imagine encountering a vast ocean current that requires repeated rowing. Loops automate this, letting you execute a block of code multiple times until a specific condition is met. The **for** loop is like a tireless oarsman, iterating over a sequence of data, executing your code for each item.

```Python
islands_to_visit = ["Isla Nublar", "Isla Sorna", "Isla Pena"]
for island in islands_to_visit:
print(f"Now approaching {island}, prepare for dinosaurs!")
# Explore each island...
```
Use code with caution.

This code loops through a list of islands, executing the exploration code for each one.

The 'while' Loop: Sailing Until Dawn

Sometimes, you set sail without a pre-defined destination, relying on the stars to guide you. The **while** loop echoes this spirit, repeating your code as long as a specific condition remains true. Think of it as an ever-vigilant lookout, checking the horizon for your target.

```
Python
sun_up = False
while not sun_up:
print("Sailing through the starry night...")
# Check for sunrise...
if is_dawn_approaching():
sun_up = True
print("Land ahoy! The sun rises on a new day!")
```
Use code with caution.

This code loops until the sun rises, simulating a night-time voyage before reaching land at dawn.

Nesting Your Options: Charts Within Charts

Just like sailing through a chain of islands, sometimes your control flow needs layers. Nested statements let you embed one control structure within another, creating intricate decision trees and dynamic program behavior.

```
Python
if difficulty == "hard":
while lives > 0:
# Gameplay loop with challenging obstacles...
if player_completes_objective():
break # Exit loop on success
else:
lives -= 1
print(f"You have {lives} lives remaining!")
if lives == 0:
print("Game over! Better luck next time.")
else:
# Easier gameplay loop...
```
Use code with caution.

This code demonstrates a nested loop within an **if** statement, creating a challenging gameplay experience on the "hard" difficulty level.

Mastering Control Flow: Charts Your Own Course

As you navigate the ocean of code, remember, control flow is your rudder. Use **if** statements to make decisions, loops to automate tasks, and nesting to create complex logic. Explore **else** and **elif** for alternative routes, and remember, practice is the key to becoming a skilled captain of your digital ship.

With these tools at your fingertips, you can chart your own course, explore uncharted territories, and leave your mark on the ever-expanding digital world. So, raise the sails.

5

functions

Having traversed the seas of control flow, we now arrive at a magnificent land: the kingdom of functions. These magical tools grant you the power to build reusable code blocks, turning complex tasks into tiny castles you can deploy across your digital realms.

Imagine crafting a spell that instantly creates a shimmering castle bridge. Functions act like that spell, encapsulating code for a specific task that you can call upon from anywhere in your program. No more repetitive building, just a single command to summon the bridge at your will!

What Do Functions Do?

Functions serve three main purposes:

1. Reduce code duplication: Instead of writing the same code multiple times, you can define a function and call it whenever needed, keeping your program clean and efficient.
2. Improve readability: Functions break down complex tasks into smaller, understandable units, making your code easier to read and maintain.
3. Increase modularity: You can group related functionality into functions, allowing you to reuse, update, and test them independently, enhancing your program's flexibility.

Building Your First Function: A Potion of Greeting

Let's brew our first function! Imagine wanting to greet everyone entering your castle. Here's how you can create a function for that:

```python
Python
def greet(name):
```

```python
    """
    This function greets the provided name with a personalized message.
    """
    print(f"Welcome, {name}, to the land of functions!")
greet("Alice") # Output: Welcome, Alice, to the land of functions!
greet("Bob") # Output: Welcome, Bob, to the land of functions!
```
Use code with caution.

This function, named **greet**, takes a single argument (**name**) and prints a personalized message. You can call it as many times as you want with different names, reusing the code without duplication.

Function Parameters: Passing Arguments into Your Castle

Just like offering ingredients to a potion, functions often require parameters. These are like drawbridges, allowing specific data to enter your function castle and be used within its code.

Our greet function can be upgraded to include an age parameter:

```python
Python
def greet(name, age):
    """
    This function greets the provided name with a personalized message based on age.
    """
    if age >= 18:
        print(f"Welcome, {name}, to the adult sector of the castle!")
    else:
        print(f"Welcome, young {name}, to the kid's zone!")
greet("Alice", 30) # Output: Welcome, Alice, to the adult sector of the castle!
greet("Bob", 12) # Output: Welcome, young Bob, to the kid's zone!
```
Use code with caution.

Now, the function uses both name and age to provide a tailored welcome based on age.

Returning Values: Bringing Treasures from Your Castle

Functions can be like treasure chambers, not just receiving data, but also giving something back. They can return values using the return keyword, sending results back to your main program.

Imagine a function that calculates the area of a rectangle:

```
Python
def area_of_rectangle(width, height):
"""
This function calculates the area of a rectangle given its width and height.
"""

area = width * height
return area
rectangle_area = area_of_rectangle(5, 10)
print(f"The area of the rectangle is: {rectangle_area}") # Output: The area of the
rectangle is: 50
```
Use code with caution.

This function takes width and height as parameters, calculates the area, and returns it to the main program, which then stores it in a variable and prints it.

Scaling Your Skills: Building Complex Function Landscapes

As you journey deeper into the land of functions, you'll encounter many more powerful concepts. From nesting functions within each other to passing functions as arguments to other functions, the possibilities are endless. Remember, practice is key! Craft new functions for common tasks, break down complex problems into smaller pieces, and let these reusable code modules strengthen your programs and enhance your coding skills.

With the power of functions at your fingertips, you can build magnificent castles of code, create modular kingdoms of functionality, and leave your mark on the ever-growing digital landscape. So, go forth, adventurer, and conquer the exciting realm of functions!

Remember:

- Define functions for reusable tasks.
- Use parameters to pass data into your functions.
- Return values from your functions for further processing.

- Nest functions and pass them as arguments to unlock advanced techniques.
- Practice crafting functions to conquer any coding challenge.

The kingdom of functions awaits! Explore its depths, unleash its power, and become a master architect.

6

lists and tuples

In our previous voyages, we've built castles with functions and steered through the seas of control flow. Now, we venture into the heart of data organization , the realm of lists and tuples, two powerful tools for storing and managing collections of information.

Imagine unearthing a forgotten treasure chest brimming with jewels, coins, and maps. Lists and tuples act like those chests, holding diverse data treasures that you can access and utilize within your programs.

Lists: Flexible Treasure Troves

Think of a list as a flexible bag, able to hold anything you throw in : numbers, strings, even other lists. It's an ordered collection, with each item occupying a specific position (index) starting from 0.

```
Python
fruits = ["apple", "banana", "orange"]
numbers = [1, 5, 7, 9]
mixed_bag = ["apple", 3.14, True]
print(fruits[1]) # Output: banana (the second fruit)
numbers.append(11) # Add a new number to the end
mixed_bag.remove("apple") # Delete an item
for fruit in fruits:
print(f"I love eating {fruit}!")
```
Use code with caution.

Lists offer amazing flexibility. You can add, remove, and modify items, iterate through them using loops, and access specific elements by their index.

Tuples: Ordered Relics

Remember that ancient scroll tucked away in the treasure chest, its contents fixed and unchangeable? Tuples resemble those relics, holding ordered collections of data like lists, but with one crucial difference : they are immutable. This means their contents cannot be modified after creation.

```
Python
dimensions = (3, 5, 10) # A tuple of three numbers
birth_date = (1990, 12, 25)
# Unpack elements into separate variables
width, height, depth = dimensions
# You cannot add, remove, or modify items in a tuple!
```
Use code with caution.

Tuples are ideal for fixed data sets like constants or measurements. They provide a sense of security, ensuring the data remains untouched by accidental modifications.

Exploring the Tools of Treasure Hunters

As you delve deeper into the world of lists and tuples, you'll discover a treasure trove of tools:

- List methods: Functions like **append**, **sort**, and **reverse** to manipulate your data.

- Tuple operations: Accessing elements by index, unpacking for convenient usage.

- List comprehensions: Powerful one-liners for creating lists based on logic.

- Nested collections: Storing lists within lists or tuples within tuples for complex data structures.

Remember, understanding the differences and choosing the right tool for the job is key to efficient and organized data management within your Python programs.

Beyond the Chests: Building Grand Libraries

With lists and tuples at your fingertips, you can build vast libraries of information, organize complex data sets, and navigate through intricate problems with ease. Think of shopping lists, user accounts, scientific datasets. The possibilities are endless!

So, polish your shovel, brave coder, and delve deeper into the treasure chambers of lists and tuples. Uncover their secrets, master their tools, and let these versatile data structures elevate your programs to new heights!

Remember:

- Lists are flexible collections of data that can be modified.

- Tuples are ordered collections that are immutable.

- Utilize list methods and tuple operations for efficient data manipulation.

- Master list comprehensions for streamlined data creation.

- Nest lists and tuples to build complex data structures.

- Choose the right tool – lists or tuples – based on your data management needs.

With lists and tuples as your allies, the world of data organization awaits your conquest!

7

dictionaries

Welcome back, intrepid traveler! We've traversed mountains of functions, sailed seas of control flow, and unearthed treasures within lists and tuples. Now, we descend into the hidden chambers of data organization, the realm of dictionaries. These magical vaults hold information not through order, but through unique keys that grant access to hidden riches.

Imagine finding a secret door in your treasure trove, leading to a chamber filled with chests, each labeled with a distinct name. Dictionaries operate similarly, storing data under specific keys instead of numbered positions. These keys act as passwords, allowing you to retrieve specific treasures instantly.

Unlocking the Vaults: Key-Value Pairs

Think of a dictionary as a collection of envelopes, each labeled with a specific name (key) and containing valuable information (value). This key-value pairing lets you access data effortlessly, without needing to remember indexes or wade through lengthy lists.

```
Python
person = {"name": "Alice", "age": 30, "job": "Programmer"}
print(person["name"]) # Output: Alice (using the key "name")
person["age"] = 31 # Update the value for "age"
for key, value in person.items():
print(f"{key}: {value}") # Loop through each key-value pair
```
Use code with caution.

Dictionaries offer tremendous flexibility. You can add, remove, and modify key-value pairs, iterate through them using loops, and access specific information with ease.

Exploring the Vaults: Hidden Structures Within

Just as a hidden chamber might contain additional secrets, dictionaries can hold nested structures like lists or even other dictionaries. This allows you to create complex data models, representing real-world entities with all their intricate details.

```
Python
inventory = {
"weapons": ["sword", "shield"],
"potions": {"health": 2, "mana": 5},
"armor": {"helmet": "steel", "chestplate": "leather"},
}
print(inventory["weapons"][1]) # Access "shield" within the "weapons" list
print(inventory["potions"]["mana"]) # Access the "mana" value within the "potions"
dictionary
```
Use code with caution.

Nested structures let you organize data hierarchically, building rich and interconnected information models within your programs.

Beyond the Keys: Mastering the Tools of Unlocking

As you dive deeper into the realm of dictionaries, you'll discover powerful tools for mastering their secrets:

- Dictionary methods: Update, delete, and check contents with functions like **update**, **pop**, and **keys.**

• Conditional access: Use **if** statements to check for specific keys before accessing values.

• Looping techniques: Iterate through keys, values, or both using various loop formats.

• Dictionary comprehensions: Build dictionaries dynamically based on logic, similar to list comprehensions.

Remember, choosing the right key structure and utilizing these tools are essential for efficient data retrieval and manipulation within your programs.

Building Grand Palaces: Information at Your Fingertips

With dictionaries as your allies, you can construct grand palaces of information. Imagine user accounts, game character stats, or intricate scientific datasets ; all organized and accessible through unique keys. These versatile vaults empower you to manage complex data effortlessly, unlocking new doors to coding possibilities.

So, gather your lockpicks, brave coder, and prepare to unravel the mysteries of dictionaries. Master their keys, unlock their hidden chambers, and let these information vaults enhance your programs to a whole new level!

Remember:

• Dictionaries store data under unique keys instead of ordered positions.

• Key-value pairs allow you to access specific information instantly.

• Dictionaries can hold nested structures like lists or other dictionaries.

- Utilize dictionary methods, conditional access, and looping techniques for efficient data manipulation.

- Master dictionary comprehensions for streamlined data creation.

- Choose the right key structure and utilize these tools to unlock the full potential of dictionaries.

With the keys of dictionaries in your hand, the grand palace of information awaits your exploration!

8

file i/o

We've journeyed through code dungeons, sailed stormy seas of data, and unlocked hidden vaults of information. Now, we stand at the threshold of an exciting frontier: the domain of file I/O[3], where your programs can venture beyond their own borders and interact with the vast digital world outside.

Imagine finding a magical portal within your castle, leading to a network of hidden libraries, each brimming with knowledge. File I/O acts as that portal, allowing your programs to read data from external files, process it, and even write their own information back to the digital landscape.

Reading Ancient Tomes: Opening and Accessing Files

Think of a file as a dusty tome within a hidden library, holding valuable information waiting to be deciphered. To access its secrets, you need the key to unlock it: the **open** function in Python.

Python
```python
file = open("treasure_map.txt", "r") # Open a file for reading
content = file.read() # Read the entire file contents
print(content) # Print the map's secrets!
file.close() # Remember to close the file afterwards!
```
Use code with caution.

This code opens a file named **"treasure_map.txt"** in read mode, storing its contents in a variable. You can then manipulate the data, analyze it, or use it within your program's logic.

Beyond Text: Exploring Diverse Formats

Your portals lead not just to dusty scrolls but to diverse libraries holding images, music, or even databases. Python offers tools to interact with various file formats:

- text files: open, read, write, and manipulate plain text data.
- image files: process images using libraries like OpenCV.
- music files: play, analyze, and manipulate audio files.
- databases: connect to databases and retrieve or store information.

Remember, each format has its own specific tools and libraries, so choose the appropriate approach based on your file type and desired operation.

Writing New Tomes: Sharing Your Discoveries

Your journey doesn't end with reading from ancient libraries. File I/O empowers you to write your own tomes, sharing your discoveries with the digital world. Use the **write** function to append or overwrite information within files.

```
Python
file = open("adventure_log.txt", "a") # Open a file for appending
file.write("Reached the hidden chamber!\n") # Add your new discoveries
file.close()
# Share your adventures with the world!
```
Use code with caution.

This code opens a file for appending and adds your latest findings to the adventure log. This allows you to create dynamic programs that interact with their environment, leaving their mark on the digital landscape.

Conquering the Unknown: Advanced File I/O Techniques

As you venture deeper into the realm of file I/O, you'll encounter new challenges and opportunities:

- Error handling: Gracefully handle errors like non-existent files or improper access.

- File paths: Navigate directory structures and locate the right files.

- Data serialization: Convert complex data structures to and from file formats.

- Threading and concurrency: Handle read/write operations efficiently with multiple threads.

Remember, practice is key! Explore different file formats, experiment with advanced techniques, and expand your skillset to conquer the complexities of file I/O.

Building Bridges to the World: Sharing Your Knowledge

File I/O doesn't just open doors to external data; it builds bridges for your programs to share their knowledge and interact with the world. Imagine writing to web servers, uploading images to social media, or reading sensor data from external devices. File I/O empowers you to create programs that connect, collaborate, and contribute to the vast digital ecosystem.

So, prepare your quill, adventurous coder, and embark on your journey through the realm of file I/O. Open portals to hidden libraries, share your discoveries with the world, and leave your mark on the ever-expanding digital landscape. Remember, the only limit is your imagination!

Remember:

- Use the **open** function to access files for reading or writing.
- Choose the appropriate mode based on your needs (read, write, append).
- Explore different file formats and their specific libraries.

- Master the **write** function to document your program's journey.
- Utilize advanced techniques like error handling and data serialization.
- Build bridges through file I/O, connecting your programs to the world.

With the power of file I/O at your fingertips, the digital landscape awaits your exploration and contribution!

9

object oriented programming (oop)

Welcome, bold architect! We've constructed sturdy code blocks, navigated through data mazes, and opened portals to external realms. Now, we ascend to a realm of transformative power: OOP. Here, you'll learn to design and create blueprints for reusable, adaptable, and interconnected components that breathe life into your digital kingdom.

Imagine a realm where every castle, every character, and every magical creature is not merely a collection of code, but a self-contained entity with its own unique properties and actions. OOP grants you the power to forge such entities, crafting a vibrant and dynamic digital world.

Blueprints for a Kingdom: Classes and Objects

At the heart of OOP lies the concept of classes. These blueprints define the structure and behavior of objects, outlining their attributes (data) and methods (functions). Think of a class as a template for crafting a specific kind of entity, like a **Warrior**, a **SpellBook**, or a **Dragon**.

Python
```python
class Dragon:
    def __init__(self, name, color, strength):
        self.name = name
        self.color = color
        self.strength = strength
    def breathe_fire(self):
        print(f"{self.name} unleashes a fiery breath!")
    def fly(self):
        print(f"{self.name} soars through the skies!")
```
Use code with caution.

This **Dragon** class defines how to create individual dragon objects, each with their own name, color, and strength.

Summoning Your Dragons: Object Instantiation

Classes are templates, but to bring their designs to life, you need to create instances, or objects, from those blueprints. This process is called instantiation.

Python

```python
smaug = Dragon("Smaug", "red", 100) # Instantiate a Dragon object named "Smaug"
smaug.breathe_fire() # Call a method on the object
smaug.fly() # Call another method
```

Use code with caution.

Each object has its own unique set of attributes, allowing you to model a diverse population of dragons, each with their own characteristics and actions.

Inheritance: Extending the Bloodline

OOP empowers you to create intricate hierarchies of classes through inheritance. Imagine a **FireDragon** class that inherits from the **Dragon** class, gaining all its attributes and methods while adding unique fire-breathing abilities.

Python

```python
class FireDragon(Dragon):
def super_fireball(self):
print(f"{self.name} unleashes a devastating super fireball!")
```

Use code with caution.

Inheritance promotes code reuse, reduces redundancy, and allows for specialized versions of classes to emerge, creating a rich tapestry of interconnected objects.

Encapsulation: Protecting the Realm's Secrets

OOP encourages encapsulation, the practice of bundling data and methods within a class, controlling access to its internal workings. This safeguards the integrity of your objects, ensuring they remain consistent and protected from unintended modifications.

Polymorphism: Many Forms, One Name

The magic of OOP lies in polymorphism, which allows objects of different classes to respond to the same method call in unique ways. Imagine a **battle** function that accepts any object capable of fighting, whether it's a **Warrior**, a **Dragon**, or a **Magician**. Each object knows how to "fight" in its own way, showcasing the adaptability and flexibility of OOP.

Building a Flourishing Kingdom: OOP in Action

OOP principles empower you to create robust, maintainable, and scalable programs. Imagine building intricate role-playing games, simulating complex ecosystems, or designing intricate user interfaces – OOP provides a structured approach to modeling real-world systems and relationships within your code.

So, grab your architect's tools, brave coder, and embark on your journey into the realm of OOP. Craft reusable blueprints, forge interconnected objects, and design a kingdom of code that thrives on adaptability, reusability, and dynamic interactions. Remember, with OOP, the only limits are your imagination and your ability to create!

10

modules and packages

Having laid the foundations with classes and objects in OOP, we now face the vastness of our own creations. As our code kingdoms grow, managing and organizing them becomes crucial. Enter the realm of modules and packages, architectural tools to bring order and clarity to your digital domain.

Imagine your magnificent castle sprawling across diverse landscapes. Modules and packages act like districts and provinces, neatly grouping related functionalities and components within your codebase.

Modules: Building Blocks of Organization

Think of a module as a self-contained unit of code, holding functions, classes, and variables relevant to a specific task or feature. It's like a well-stocked workshop specializing in a particular craft, keeping your code organized and modular.

```python
Python
# In a file named "magic_spells.py"
def fireball(target):
print(f"A fiery blast engulfs {target}!")
def healing_touch(target):
print(f"{target} feels a surge of restorative energy!")
```
Use code with caution.

This module, named "magic_spells.py", houses functions for casting spells, encapsulating those functionalities within a specific unit.

Importing Magic: Bringing Resources into Your Castle

To utilize the spells from your magic workshop, you need to **import** them into your main program. Think of it as sending messengers from your castle to fetch the desired tools.

```python
Python
# In your main program
```

```
import magic_spells
spellcaster = "Merlin"
magic_spells.fireball("dragon")
magic_spells.healing_touch(spellcaster)
```
Use code with caution.

By importing the "magic_spells" module, you gain access to its functions within your program, allowing you to cast spells at will.

Packages: Grand Districts of Code

While modules focus on specific tasks, packages act as larger districts, grouping multiple modules under a single banner. Imagine a grand province dedicated to magic, encompassing various workshops for spells, enchantments, and magical creatures.

```
Python
# Create a package directory named "wizardry"
- magic_spells.py
- magical_creatures.py
- enchantment_recipes.py
# Package name becomes "wizardry"
```
Use code with caution.

By grouping related modules into a package, you create a clear hierarchy and reduce clutter, making your codebase easier to navigate and understand.

Advantages of a Well-Organized Realm

The benefits of utilizing modules and packages are vast:

- Reduced code duplication: Share common functionalities across modules and packages.

- Improved code readability: Group related code with clear purpose and structure.

- Enhanced maintainability: Update or replace modules without affecting the entire program.

- Increased modularity: Reuse modules and packages across different projects.

- Simplified collaboration: Share code efficiently within teams.

By embracing these organizational tools, you transform your sprawling codebase into a well-structured empire, allowing you and others to navigate and maintain your creations with ease.

Exploring the Frontiers: Advanced Packaging Techniques

As you delve deeper into the realm of modules and packages, you'll encounter powerful techniques:

- Packages within packages: Create nested structures for intricate organization.

- Sub-packages: Group related modules within packages for further granularity.

- Importing specific functions: Import only the needed functions from a module.

- Naming conventions: Follow best practices for consistent and easy-to-understand names.

Remember, mastering these techniques takes practice and exploration. Experiment with different structures, explore existing open-source packages, and refine your organizational skills to become a true master of code architecture.

Building an Enduring Legacy: Sharing Your Creations

Modules and packages empower you not only to manage your own code but also to share your creations with the world. Imagine publishing your magic modules to online repositories, allowing other programmers to cast spells and build upon your foundations.

By contributing to the vast ecosystem of open-source libraries and modules, you leave a lasting legacy, making your code not just a kingdom, but a bridge to connect and inspire others.

So, take hold of the organizational tools of modules and packages, architect your codebases with precision, and share your creations with the world. Remember, a well-organized and documented digital empire stands the test of time, leaving a lasting mark on the ever-evolving landscape of code.

Remember:

- Modules group related functionalities and code into self-contained units.

- Use import statements to bring module functionalities into your program.

- Packages act as larger districts, grouping related modules under a single banner.

- Leverage modules and packages to improve code organization, readability, and maintainability.

- Explore advanced techniques like nested packages, sub-packages, and specific function imports.

- Share your modules and packages to contribute to the open-source community.

11

errors and handling

Welcome back, intrepid adventurer! We've explored castles of functions, sailed seas of data, and built empires of modules. Now, we venture into the inevitable territory ; the realm of errors and handling. Imagine your magnificent journey encountering unexpected twists and turns, but fear not! Mastering error handling equips you with the tools to navigate these bumps and ensure your programs reach their destination.

Think of errors like hidden cracks in your castle walls, threatening its stability. Unhandled errors can crash your programs, leaving you bewildered and your users frustrated. But with error handling techniques, you transform these cracks into stepping stones, gracefully recovering from unexpected situations and ensuring your digital journey continues uninterrupted.

Unmasking the Shadows: Common Error Types

Errors come in various forms, each requiring specific remedies:

- Syntax errors: Typos, missing punctuation, or incorrect grammar in your code.

- Runtime errors: Issues that occur while your program is running, like missing variables or incompatible data types.

- Logical errors: Mistakes in your program's logic, leading to incorrect results or unintended behavior.

By understanding these types, you can anticipate potential glitches and prepare your defenses.

Building Your Guard Towers: Exception Handling

Exception handling acts as your guard towers, constantly vigilant for errors. You use **try** and **except** blocks to catch unforeseen challenges and provide alternative paths for your program to take.

```python
Python
try:
# Try to run your code here
divide_by_zero = 10 / 0
except ZeroDivisionError:
print("Division by zero is not allowed!")
else:
print("Everything went smoothly!")
```
Use code with caution.

Here, the **try** block attempts the division. If a **ZeroDivisionError** occurs, the **except** block takes over, printing a message instead of crashing. The **else** block runs only if no errors occur.

Fortifying Your Walls: Different Exception Types

You can catch specific errors using their exact names within the **except** block:

```python
Python
try:
# Code using file
file = open("missing_file.txt", "r")
except FileNotFoundError:
print("The file could not be found!")
except PermissionError:
print("You don't have permission to access the file!")
```
Use code with caution.

This code catches both **FileNotFoundError** and **PermissionError** separately, providing tailored responses to each potential issue.

Raising the Alarm: Custom Exceptions

Sometimes, you need to raise the alarm even before encountering an error. Use the **raise** keyword to throw a custom exception, alerting your program and triggering appropriate handling:

```
Python
def withdraw_money(amount):
if amount > balance:
raise InsufficientFundsError("Not enough money in your account!")
# Update balance and return remaining amount
```
Use code with caution.

This function raises a custom **InsufficientFundsError** if the requested withdrawal exceeds the account balance, allowing for specific handling of this scenario.

Beyond the Walls: Robust and Informative Errors

Remember, effective error handling goes beyond just preventing crashes:

- Provide informative messages: Clearly explain what went wrong to help you and users debug the issue.

- Log errors: Save details of the error for later analysis and improvement.

- Offer recovery options: If possible, present users with alternatives or ways to continue.

By embracing these practices, you transform errors from roadblocks into valuable feedback, learning opportunities, and ultimately, tools to strengthen your programs and enhance the user experience.

Conquering the Unexpected: Embracing Error Handling

With error handling skills at your disposal, you can navigate the unpredictable terrain of code with confidence. Embrace the bumps, anticipate the twists, and build programs that adapt, recover, and continue their journey even when faced with the unexpected. Remember, the mark of a skilled coder is not only building flawless code, but also crafting programs that gracefully handle the inevitable hiccups along the way.

So, raise your shield of awareness, equip yourself with the tools of exception handling, and embark on your digital adventures with the knowledge that no error can truly stop you. The road may be bumpy, but your programs will emerge stronger, more resilient, and ready to conquer any challenge!

Remember:

- Understand different error types: Syntax, runtime, and logical errors.

- Utilize try-except blocks for exception handling.

- Catch specific errors using their names or raise custom exceptions.

- Provide informative messages and logging for error analysis.

- Offer recovery options and graceful error handling for best user experience.

With these tools in your arsenal, you can navigate the realm of errors with confidence and emerge victorious!

12

project: build a web scraper

So far in this journey, we've traversed mountains of knowledge, sailed turbulent seas of data, and conquered the treacherous realm of errors. Now, we embark on a thrilling expedition: building a web scraper! Imagine venturing into the vast digital ocean, wielding the tools of Python to extract hidden treasures from the depths of the web.

Think of websites as treasure chests brimming with information, guarded by HTML and CSS locks. Your quest, armed with Python libraries like **requests** and **BeautifulSoup**, is to unlock these chests, extract the valuable data within, and transform it into a useful bounty.

Charting Your Course: Defining the Target and Scrape Goal

Your adventure begins with a clear objective. Identify the website you want to scrape and choose the specific data you seek. Do you desire book titles from an online bookstore, news headlines from a specific source, or product prices from a shopping website? Define your target and map your extraction route accordingly.

Python

```
# Target website: https://www.examplebookstore.com/bestsellers
# Desired data: Book titles and authors
Use code with caution.
```

This example sets the target website and identifies the two data points you want to extract.

Setting Sail: Tools and Libraries for Scrapyard Success

Stock your digital ship with powerful tools:

- **requests**: Sends HTTP requests to download website content.
- **BeautifulSoup**: Parses HTML content, making it easier to extract data.
- **lxml**: A fast and efficient HTML parser (optional, but recommended).

```python
Python
import requests
from bs4 import BeautifulSoup
Use code with caution.
```

These libraries allow you to access, navigate, and extract information from the website's HTML code.

Diving into the Depths: Locating Your Treasure

Once you have landed on your target island (downloaded the website content), it's time to hunt for your treasure. Use **BeautifulSoup** to find the HTML elements containing your desired data. Think of these elements as hidden compartments within the chest, holding the information you seek.

```python
Python
soup = BeautifulSoup(content, "lxml")
# Find all elements containing book titles
book_elements = soup.find_all("h2", class_="book-title")
# Extract titles and authors from each element
for element in book_elements:
title = element.text.strip()
author = element.find("span", class_="author").text.strip()
print(f"Title: {title}, Author: {author}")
Use code with caution.
```

This code identifies all "h2" elements with the class "book-title", which likely hold the book titles. It then loops through these elements, extracting the title and author information from each and printing it to the console.

Plundering the Spoils: Storing and Utilizing Your Data

With your data extracted, it's time to secure it! Store the information in a structured format like a list or dictionary for further analysis or usage. You can then write the data to a file, display it in a graphical user interface (GUI), or analyze it with other Python tools.

```
Python
books = []
for element in book_elements:
title = element.text.strip()
author = element.find("span", class_="author").text.strip()
books.append({"title": title, "author": author})
# Save the list of books to a file
with open("bestsellers.csv", "w") as f:
writer = csv.writer(f)
writer.writerow(["Title", "Author"])
for book in books:
writer.writerow([book["title"], book["author"]])
```
Use code with caution.

This code demonstrates storing the extracted data in a list of dictionaries and then writing it to a CSV file for further use.

Navigating the Stormy Seas: Ethical Scrapyard Practices

Remember, web scraping carries ethical responsibilities:

- Respect **robots.txt**: Always check and obey robots exclusion protocols.

- Be mindful of server load: Don't overload website servers with excessive scraping.

- Extract data responsibly: Don't scrape sensitive information or harm the website's functionality.

Responsible scraping ensures a sustainable and ethical digital exploration.

Charting New Courses: Beyond Basic Scraping

This project is just the tip of the iceberg! Explore advanced techniques:

- Handling dynamic content: Use **JavaScript** rendering libraries like **Selenium**.

- Scraping complex websites: Employ advanced parsing techniques and regular expressions.

- Building robust scraping frameworks: Create reusable code and handle errors gracefully.

Remember, the possibilities are endless! With knowledge, practice, and ethical principles, you can become a master digital treasure hunter, extracting valuable information from the web and enriching your own programming journey.

13

project: create a simple game

Welcome back, intrepid coder! We've ventured through coding caves, sailed data seas, and unearthed treasures of knowledge. I'm personally addicted to Candy Crush Saga[4], and I've been playing it for years! It all starts with the basics, so let's embark on a playful expedition: creating a simple game! Imagine crafting your own interactive world, where lines of code transform into pixelated characters and challenges, beckoning players to join the fun.

Think of a game as a miniature digital universe, governed by your own rules and fueled by your creativity. With Python libraries like **Pygame** at your fingertips, you can bring your playful visions to life, pixel by pixel, animation by animation.

Defining the Playground: Choosing Your Game Genre and Mechanics

Your journey begins with a spark of inspiration. Will you build a thrilling platform, a brain-teasing puzzle game, or a retro-inspired arcade adventure? Choose a genre and define the core mechanics – how will players interact with your world, what are the goals, and what challenges will they face?

```
Python
# Defining a simple "Space Invaders" inspired game
# Player controls a spaceship at the bottom of the screen
# Shoot lasers to destroy descending alien invaders
# Earn points for each alien destroyed
# Game ends when all aliens are defeated or player loses all lives
```

Use code with caution.

This example outlines a basic "Space Invaders" inspired game, setting the stage for further development.

Building the Blocks: Setting Up Your Game Environment

With your playground defined, it's time to lay the foundation. Install **Pygame** and utilize its modules to set up your game window, handle graphics, and manage user input.

```python
Python
import pygame
# Initialize Pygame and create window
pygame.init()
screen = pygame.display.set_mode((800, 600))
# Define colors and fonts
BLACK = (0, 0, 0)
WHITE = (255, 255, 255)
# Create player spaceship and alien sprites
player_sprite = pygame.image.load("player.png")
alien_sprite = pygame.image.load("alien.png")
```
Use code with caution.

This code initializes **Pygame**, creates a window, defines basic colors and fonts, and loads images for the player and alien sprites.

Bringing the World to Life: Drawing, Updating, and Responding

Now, let your digital canvas come alive! Use **Pygame** functions to draw sprites, update the game state, and respond to player input. Implement a game loop that constantly refreshes the screen and reacts to user actions.

```python
Python
# Game loop
running = True
while running:
# Check for events and player input
for event in pygame.event.get():
if event.type == pygame.QUIT:
running = False
# Update game state and positions
player_y = player_y + move_y
```

```
# Draw sprites and background
screen.fill(BLACK)
screen.blit(player_sprite, (player_x, player_y))
screen.blit(alien_sprite, (alien_x, alien_y))
# Update the display
pygame.display.flip()
# Quit Pygame
pygame.quit()
```
Use code with caution.

This simple loop checks for events and updates the game state based on player input. It then draws the player and alien sprites on the screen before refreshing the display.

Adding Layers of Fun: Animations, Sound Effects, and Levels

Remember, the magic lies in the details! Enhance your game with:

- Animations: Breathe life into your sprites with movement and effects.

- Sound effects: Add audio cues for actions, impacts, and background music.

- Levels: Introduce difficulty progression, new challenges, and unlockable content.

Each addition deepens player engagement and keeps them coming back for more.

Sharing Your Creation: Release Your Playful Masterpiece

Let the world enjoy your playground! Consider platforms like **itch.io** to share your game with others, gather feedback, and fuel your creative journey. Even a simple game can bring joy and spark inspiration in others.

So, unleash your inner game designer, embrace the playful possibilities of Python, and build your own pixelated wonderland. With each line of code, you sculpt a world of challenge, amusement, and the endless satisfaction of creating something truly your own. Remember, the playground is yours to build, the rules are yours to define, and the fun is just a keystroke away!

Don't forget:

- Choose a game genre and define core mechanics.
- Set up your game environment with Pygame.
- Implement a game loop for ongoing updates and player interaction.
- Add layers of fun with animations, sound effects, and levels.
- Share your creation with the world

14

next steps in python

Welcome, fellow adventurer! We've traversed mountains of concepts, sailed through seas of code, conquered realms of errors, and crafted playful digital playgrounds. Now, we stand at the edge of an expansive world, ready to embark on our next grand expedition – exploring the vast possibilities that Python offers!

Imagine a realm where your programming skills merge with diverse domains, opening doors to exciting new adventures and meaningful creations. This chapter serves as a compass, guiding you toward captivating destinations and empowering you to chart your unique path within the Python landscape.

Expanding Your Horizons: Discovering New Domains

- Data Science and Machine Learning: Unleash the power of Python to analyze datasets, uncover hidden patterns, and build intelligent systems that learn and adapt.

- Web Development: Craft dynamic and interactive websites using Python frameworks like **Django** and **Flask**.

- Automation and Scripting: Streamline tasks, automate workflows, and simplify complex processes with Python scripts.

- Game Development: Create immersive games, from simple arcade classics to elaborate 3D worlds, using libraries like **Pygame** and **PyOpenGL**.

- Scientific Computing: Handle complex mathematical computations and create visualizations for scientific analysis.

- Network Programming: Build applications that communicate over networks, enabling features like chat systems, file transfers, and web services.

- Artificial Intelligence: Explore the frontiers of AI, building intelligent agents, chatbots, and machine learning models.

- And beyond! Python's versatility extends to robotics, bioinformatics, education, finance, and countless other fields.

Charting Your Course: Choosing Your Path

1. Follow Your Passions: Align your Python journey with your interests and goals. What problems spark your curiosity? What domains captivate your imagination?

1. Explore Resources and Communities: Immerse yourself in books, tutorials, online courses, and communities like those on **GitHub** and **Stack Overflow**.
2. Practice Consistently: Build projects, experiment with code, and learn from your mistakes.
3. Contribute to Open-Source Projects: Collaborate with others, gain experience, and give back to the community.
4. Seek Mentorship and Guidance: Connect with experienced developers for advice and support.

Strengthening Your Craft: Skills to Embrace

- Object-Oriented Programming (OOP): Master object-oriented concepts to structure your code effectively and create reusable components.

- Data Structures and Algorithms: Choose the right data structures and algorithms to solve problems efficiently.

- Testing and Debugging: Write comprehensive tests to ensure code quality and learn to debug efficiently.

- Version Control: Use **Git** or similar tools to track code changes and collaborate effectively.

- Design Patterns: Learn common solutions to recurring programming problems.

- Best Practices: Adopt coding conventions and best practices for maintainability and readability.

Embracing the Journey: Continuous Learning and Growth

Remember, Python mastery is a lifelong adventure. Embrace curiosity, challenge yourself, and never stop learning. Embrace challenges, persevere through setbacks, and celebrate your accomplishments. The path ahead is boundless, filled with exciting possibilities and endless potential. Forge your own unique journey in the world of Python, and let your code leave a lasting impact on the world.

So, pack your bags, fellow explorer, and let's venture forth into the limitless realm of Python possibilities! The world awaits your creations!

---

[1] Python programming language is older than Java

[2] PEMDAS stands for parenthesis, exponents, multiplication, division, addition, subtraction

[3] input/output file operations

[4] game created by of **KING**, a video game development company founded by *Ricardo Zacconi* and that generates on average a whooping **1.1 billion USD** revenue annually !!

Don't miss out!

Visit the website below and you can sign up to receive emails whenever Eric Sindeu publishes a new book. There's no charge and no obligation.

https://books2read.com/r/B-A-EXKCB-TXXSC

BOOKS2READ

Connecting independent readers to independent writers.

About the Author

About the Author

Eric Sindeu, Sr. Telecom Engineer, is a Cameroonian born on July 24th 1975. He is an entrepreneur as well as the founder and current CEO of KEMITEL, a digital company aiming to provide innovative and affordable digital services across Africa. He has acquired skills over the years on several technologies and services including cloud computing, IoT, satellite communications, fintech and digital coding.70 He received the 2022 Africa Innovation Award by African Alliance of ICT organizations. Eric is a proud father of two children and a sports avid sports fan (American Football, Basketball, Soccer).

www.ingramcontent.com/pod-product-compliance
Lightning Source LLC
Chambersburg PA
CBHW061338120726
48001CB00002B/918